Hip. Hip. Hallelujah!

DR. JOHN DEE JEFFRIES

EDITED BY C. GENEVIEVE JEFFRIES

Author of The Last Martyr; and, When I Can't Find God

VOLUME 2

Hip. Hip. Hallelujah!
Volume 2
Copyright © John Dee Jeffries
Author of The Last Martyr; When I Can't Find God and
Hip. Hip. Hallelujah! Volume 1, 2 & 3

Published By Parables

All Rights Reserved. No part of this book may be reproduced or utilized in any form or by any means, electronic or mechanical, including photocopying, recording, or by any information storage and retrieval system, without permission in writing from the author.

Unless otherwise specified Scripture quotations are taken from the authorized version of the King James Bible.

First Edition   June, 2017

ISBN 978-1-945698-13-2

Printed in the United States of America

Readers should be aware that Internet Web sites offered as citations and/or sources for further information may have been changed or disappeared between the time this was written and when it is read.

Illustration provided by www.unsplash.com

Hip. Hip. Hallelujah!

DR. JOHN DEE JEFFRIES
EDITED BY C. GENEVIEVE JEFFRIES

Author of The Last Martyr; and, When I Can't Find God

VOLUME 2

PUBLISHED by PARABLES
Earthly Stories with a Heavenly Meaning

God's Kisses

I hope you see God in these stories! Each of these stories are true! Definitely! In my mind it is here, in our stories, that inspiration, inspired interpretation and imagination meet in miraculous ways.

By the way, in the Bible, when God does His thing, we call them "miracles" – today, people call them "God Things" (when God does something miraculous).

I call them "God's Kisses" – and that young mother and that little boy – God kissed 'em! He did! And, hey, listen, as I write this, know this, I have Divine Lipstick smeared all over me! And so do you! Nothing can separate me and nothing can separate you from the love of God!

God's kisses!
Hip! Hip! Hallelujah!

JOHN DEE JEFFRIES

May God kiss you through these stories – even as He has kissed me!

Hip. Hip.
Hallelujah!

Now, what's that smudge
of red on your cheek?

A Vital Question
Are these stories true?

We began volume one of the Hip. Hip. Hallelujah series by refering to what many today call "God-Things." These are the things that God and only God can do. We begin this second volume with the same reference to "God'Things."

I hope you see God in these stories! Each of these stories are true! Definitely! They really did happen!

In the Bible, when God does His thing, we call them "miracles." Today people call them "God Things" ("God Things" are when God does something miraculous).

I call them "God's Kisses" – hey, listen, as I write this I have Divine Lipstick smeared all over me! No kidding! And so do you!

Remember, Nothing can separate me and nothing can separate you from the love of God! Nothing.

True stories – "truth spoken in love!"

Hip! Hip! Hallelujah!

May God kiss you through these stories even as He has kissed me! Now, what's that smudge of red on your cheek.

2nd verse, same as the first --
Hip! Hip! Hallelujah!

An Unspeakable Opportunity!
God Doesn't Forget The Future

Even heroes have flat tires, or so I'm told. Experience reveals that regular salt-of-the-earth folk have their share of flat tires too! Poets turn flat tires into metaphors – filled with hidden meanings that tickle the imagination. Ordinary folk, however, seldom see beyond the grime and hassle of lug nuts, tire jacks – and the flatness of the tire.

Which brings me to Adolph! (And a few others). Long ago, during a long hot month of June, God used Adolph – in a strange, metaphorical way, in a way that was filled with hidden mystery and meaning!

"Adolph bought new tires," said mom in a long distance telephone conversation. I was a second year Bible student at Clarke College in Mississippi. Mom was back home in New

Orleans. Adolph was a neighbor who lived, like most of us did back then, in a shot-gun New Orleans camel back house.

"Adolph bought new tires," said mom, "and he kept the four he replaced for you!"

So, a couple of weeks later I piled four nearly new spare tires in the wash room of the parsonage (preacher's house) and I forgot about that. (God didn't!)

Two days later I received a telephone call from a young fella' in the church. "Pastor," says he, "I bought me a new set of tires – and kept the four that I replaced for you! I'm five minutes away."

He and I piled four nearly new spare tires in the wash room of the parsonage and I forgot about that. (God didn't!)

Now here's a strange thing. For the next couple of months people kept giving me their replacement tires. The washroom had roughly twenty-five spare tires crammed as high as the ceiling. (It looked like a tire warehouse).

I repeatedly forgot about those tires, however. Out of sight; out of mind. (My wife didn't forget, however. She was constantly stepping around tires every wash day! Yipes! And, of course -- God didn't forget either.).

No! God didn't forget. He didn't forget the future! When we forget our forgetfulness is rooted in the past. It is impossible for us to forget the future because it is impossible to forget the unknown -- impossible to forget things that have not yet happened! Adolph? These tires! In a strange, mysterious way God was letting me in on a secret – God doesn't forget the future!

"Honey," says I one day, sounding like an inspired prophet, "Honey, we're going to have a lot of flat tires this school year."

And – we did! Not one of those twenty-something spare tires were left at the end of the school year.

And God? Well, I'm so glad God didn't forget the future!

Hip! Hip! Hallelujah!

Who Woulda' Thunk It?
God! That's Who!

Decisions! We make them everyday! Some are large! Some are small! Or, are they? The year? 1992. I began my doctoral studies at the New Orleans Baptist Theological Seminary (A great seminary, by the way!) At some point I had to choose a doctoral project

Hmmmm!

My project eventually bore the title – "A Program For Developing And Reinforcing Values In the Weekday Preschool Of First Baptist Church, Chalmette, Louisiana." (Goodness! That's a mouthful!)

I chose that area of study with a focus on the needs of 1992. We had a weekday preschool at First Baptist, Chalmette, a really good one! Nevertheless, without any thought for the future the doctrinal project was completed and I received my doctoral degree!

Through the years many people asked, "Why did you focus on the work of a Weekday Preschool?" Quite honestly, I never really had an answer – I just felt led!

Fast Forward! The year? 2005. Hurricane Katrina. Everything was lost. Our home. Our community. Our church. Our weekday preschool. Slowly, very slowly, our church limped to recovery. Eventually, the day came. Our new building was completed. A year later we resurrected and reopened the Weekday Preschool of First Baptist Church. Enrollment soared! So much so that we could not continue to expand unless we became a licensed preschool. We met the criteria and satisfied the prerequisites to receive our license with the state of Louisiana – sort of! Even though we had then and still have an excellent, fully-trained, certified staff, no one fully met the stringent demands of the Louisiana Department of Education to serve as Executive Director of the Weekday Preschool. Two or three of our staff were close, very close, but not quite close enough!

Hey! Remember back in 1992. I chose that area of study with a focus on the needs of 1992. I made that decision without any thought for the future. I had no idea that God intentionally guided that decision back in 1992 with His eye on the future – 2009

God is always active in our present. We know He is here, there, everywhere – all the time always present in our present! Tomorrow, or next week, or next year, something may intrude into the flow of our lives. Get this! God is here, with us today, guiding our decisions and He is already there – in the future -- making preparations and provisions for us – to overcome the challenges that are there!

Sing this loudly, please. Congratulations, to me! Congratulations, to me! I'm the pastor? Yep! And, I'm the Executive Director of the Weekday Preschool too! Go on….. Fully-Qualified because of, what's the name of that doctoral project….?

Hip! Hip! Hallelujah!

Decisions! We make them everyday!
Decisions! God makes/made them too!

In eternity past, before the world was created, God saw every person who would ever live. He saw every generation, every period of history, every moment in time. He saw every circumstance and every situation that would ever come into existence.

It's important for us to realize that nothing – nothing in your life or my life – nothing ever catches God by surprise. He sees what's coming, makes provision both before and as it comes into existence, and interjects Himself into the situation and accomplishes His redemptive purpose – even in the midst of the most turbulent events, unpleasant situations and difficult times.

To illustrate, let's think about you. Science

tells us that, like snowflakes, no two people are alike. Each person possesses a special uniqueness that makes them distinct from every other person. Implication: You're special! You – yes, you – you possess a special uniqueness! No one that ever lived before, no one that lives today and no one that lives tomorrow will ever think, feel, dream, walk or even talk exactly like you! No one else has your mind, your heart, your eyes, your ears, your hands, your mouth or your body. You possess a special uniqueness that makes you distinct and different from everybody else. That uniqueness makes you who you are – someone special in the eyes of God!

And, God saw you, gifted with that special uniqueness that makes you who you are, even before the world was created, even before you had existence and He loved you. Then God looked at all of the various countries in the world that would ever have existence and He loved them. He loved their uniqueness. He loved their people. God also looked at all the periods of human history and based on His love, He decided "when" an "where" you should live and have existence! (Acts 17:24-26, notice v. 26)

You see, God has a special purpose and a special plan for you and your life, based on His love for you, your uniqueness and the uniqueness of these times. And, through His love He has actually been negotiating circumstances to draw you to Him and to His special purpose and plan for your life.

Our goal in life – your goal and my goal – is not to decide what we want to do but to discover what He has purposed, planned and destined us to do!

Sometimes, that means a guy like me – a simple pastor -- becomes the Executive Director of the Weekday Preschool too! Go on…..

Hip! Hip! Hallelujah!

Weary Fishermen!
The BP Oil Crisis

The BP Oil Crisis! The Gulf of Mexico. 35 miles away. 4 a.m. The BP staging area. Twice a week a group of men and women huddled together as I led them in prayer.

"Why do you come to pray with us," asked a weary fishermen.

"I come because there is a God and He hears and answers prayer!"

"I'm about to lose my boat," says he. "Would you pray for me!" I held his hand and did just that.

Twenty minutes later my cell phone rang.

"You don't know me and I don't know you. I live in California and I just watched a news report about the plight of the poor fishermen and the hurt that this catastrophe was causing them. God told me to payoff the balance on a fishermen's boat. Can you help me with that?"

"Yes. I can. I was just with him."

Eleven days later I handed a $11,000.00 check to an astonished fishermen and his wife.

What's with you? What's your problem? Know this: There is a God and He hears and answers prayer!

Hip! Hip! Hallelujah!

Play Ball
That's the way the ball bounces!

That's the way the ball bounces! This everyday phrase is often used when someone has decided to accept the unacceptable outcome of an unpleasant situation. It's a cliché used to explain the idea that there are some things that we cannot control and once they have happened, we have to live with the consequences – even if we don't like the consequences.

Here's a faith builder: Wherever you find yourself, whether it's at the top of the mountain or in the depths of the deepest valley, God is there, and because He cares for you, you can live courageously, even if you don't like the way the ball bounces.

So, the next time you find your courage

tested to the limit, the next time you're angry and disappointed, the next time the ball takes a bad bounce, remember this, God is as near as your next breath. And He hears and answers prayer! Play ball!

Hip! Hip! Hallelujah!

The Flea Market
Too Busy For God!

The place smelled terrible! Musty! Stale! Moldy! A rickety rotating fan strained to overcome the excessive heat! There was no air conditioning! Just the fan! And, there he sat – surrounded by junk! All kinds of junk! Stuff was stacked ceiling high! Against the walls – all of the walls! In big piles at the center of each room! Junk was everywhere! "I've got two other stores just like this one," he said proudly, surrounded by his junk. "Flea markets! I call them indoor flea markets!"

My visitation partner and I shared our faith using every soul-winning method and technique possible – without success!

"I appreciate you coming," said he, "I really do; but, I don't have time for the Bible and church stuff. I'm just too busy, you know. I've got two other stores just like this one!" Just as I reached the door I turned and said, "Thanks for the hospitality and the warm welcome. But, there is one last thing I have to say!"

"And, what might that be," says he.

"Mister, you're the first man I've ever met who had the guts to say he was too busy for God!"

The following Sunday the church was packed with people. Wonderful music! Preaching! Then, the most exciting part – the invitation! People were receiving Christ, coming forward. The invitation was about to close when…

The little man from the flea market store came forward!

"After you guys left I thought about what I'd said," said he. "Then, later that night as I lay in bed I thought about what you said…

"Mister, you're the first man I've ever met who had the guts to say he was too busy for God!"

With a tear at the corner of each eye he said, "It wasn't guts, it was stupidity. As I lay in bed I heard myself described as a man too busy for God….too busy for God….too busy for God. As I looked back over my life it's always been that way – to busy!"

A few years later he was serving Christ as the Chairman of Deacons!

Hip. Hip, Hallelujah!

Business
Distractions and Diversionns

I can appreciate the frustration Charlie Brown has in the Peanuts cartoons. Like the one where Lucy is philosophizing and Charlie is listening. As usual, Lucy has the floor, delivering one of her lectures.

She says, "Charlie Brown, life is a lot like a deck chair. Some place it so they can see where they're going. Others place it to see where they've been. And some so they can see where they are at the present."

Charlie Brown sighs and says, "I can't even get mine unfolded."

More than a few of us can identify with Charlie Brown. Life gets rough at times. Some of the choices we have to make are difficult. We find ourselves, like the old saying, "between a rock and a hard place." Stuck between two possibilities where an argument can be made for going either way. We have a name for this type of situation – dilemma!

Whenever we're faced with a dilemma we're pulled in two different directions. We feel the strain and we don't quite know what's the best thing to do. And, I might add, being older and wiser doesn't mean that you're immune to the problem.. As Charlie Brown put it, there are times when we find difficult to get our deck chair unfolded.

When we encounter a dilemma and we're unable to figure out the right direction, it's very important that we turn to God's Word for guidance – we need to hear His voice! There are a lot of different voices all around us, trying to pull us in different directions. Some of them are loud, some are persuasive and a few are down right convincing. It can be confusing. If you listen long enough to the wrong voices you may be tempted to throw your faith to the wind, look out for number one and make a wrong choice.

So, here's a good place to start. Slow down. Push the busyness aside. Put everything on hold. Then, go to the Word of God, pray, read James 1:5, then allow God to lead you. He will! Count on it!

We live in a world that is full of…

> Busyness   Noise
> Clatter   Distractions
> Diversions   Disruptions

So much so that many people are…
> Unable to hear the still, small voice of God as He speaks

Question   What about you?

> Are you hearing God speak to you?
> Are you tuned in to God's voice?

Do you hear Him when He speaks to you?

Just as God, at sundry times and in divers manners spake in time PAST God still speaks TODAY

Question: How Does God Speak Today?

We live in a…..
> Crowded World   Noisy World
> Competing Voices   Distractions
> Diversions   Distortions

> A World where many find it difficult to hear God

JOHN DEE JEFFRIES

We want to…
>   Hear from God
>   Know what is on God's mind
>   Know His agenda for our lives

Here are Four Ways God Speaks to us…

>   Circumstances of Life
>   Word of God
>   People of God
>   Spirit of God

>   Hip. Hip, Hallelujah!

Catch Me. Please Catch Me.
Will You Be Made Whole? Part 1

"Bulimia," says she. "I've had it for years and I've tried just about everything and been just about everywhere to get this monkey off my back. You're the end of the road for me. I have no one else to turn to and no where else to go."

She described a long litany of inpatient and outpatient treatment centers, recovery programs, books she'd read, seminars she'd attended, etc. –all to no avail!

A few things about her are etched in memory. First, I shared with her that her hope was in Christ and in Christ alone! Second, as her counseling progressed I gave her a written assignment. "Write a few brief sentences about each of the following, then add some concluding remarks: The Miracle Of Me, The Master Of Me, The Mystery Of Me and The Misery Of Me then Concluding Remarks."

She did that assignment, with an inordinate preoccupation that focused on "The Misery Of Me" that ended with the following concluding sentence: "Dear God, in misery, I am running away from You as fast as I can. Please catch me. Please."

Anyone can run away from God – Jonah, Ezekiel and a host of others tried it -- without success! Jonah prayed to God from the belly of the fish, saying, "I called out to the Lord, out of my distress, and he answered me." Ezekiel, exhausted and in despair heard that special still voice of God while hiding in a cave.

Are you running from God? Many people try, but it's impossible! We simply can't run from an omnipresent God. It's impossible?

David indicated this when he wrote: "Where shall I go from your Spirit? Or where shall I flee from your presence? If I ascend to heaven, you are there! If I make my bed in Sheol, you are there! If I take the wings of the morning and dwell in the uttermost parts of the sea, even there your hand shall lead me, and your 'right' hand shall hold me."

"Dear God, in misery, I am running away

from You as fast as I can. Please catch me. Please."

Hip. Hip. Hallelujah

Catch Me. Please Catch Me.
Will You Be Made Whole? Part 2

Some folks say "If I knew then what I know now!" But, suppose we reverse that – "If I knew now what I knew then!"

Memory is selective. It sorts and categories every event and every life experience – not haphazardly, nor with hesitation – but with intent and purpose! While cognitive intent and purpose vary, guided by many forces and governed by many factors – one primary purpose of the categorization is self-protection.

Self-protection extends beyond mere physical survival – and encompasses the emotional component as well! Sometimes, the avoidance of pain and the sting of self-confrontation are so strong that distortion occurs – and we reshape the events and life-experiences of the past! This is why the Bible warns us about the "deceitfulness" of man and the "deceitfulness" of the human heart!

The "deceitfulness" of man! Have you ever noticed that when you're reading a book or watching a movie – you always identify with the hero, the good guy, the guy who wins in the end! You don't see the villain as you – the villain simply is not and cannot be you! Why? Well, because he's a villain! The bad guy is not you either – the bad guy is not and cannot be you! Why? Well, because he's a bad guy. Me? A bad guy? Definitely not! Nope! Not me! I'm not the villain… I'm not the bad guy!

Now, think about this – then, the next time your mind acts like a television and you watch a "rerun" of a real life events or experience, the end of the story may be based more on what is now than what was back then when the event or life experience occurred!

Forgetfulness, by the way, is often an emotional tool that is used to minimize pain. Sometimes forgetfulness will even deny pains existence. We re-shuffle, then reshape events, then we watch our mental version of "what was" then we rerun that mental version again. We do this re-shuffle/reshape/

rerun again, and again, and again….

And, then, like the Prodigal Son who – came unto himself – and we see the root of our misery – The Misery of Me – and we cry out to God…

"Dear God, in misery, I am running away from You as fast as I can. Please catch me. Please."

Hip. Hip. Hallelujah

Stop Digging!
The First Rule Of Holes!

Just left the home of a young couple raised in the faith. A disappointing visit. One of their children had invited Jesus into their little heart. Such childlike faith. Tears and joy were two of several indicators that the child really understood the implications of the decision – and the child was eager to follow Jesus in believer's baptism

"Well, we don't go to church much anymore," said one parent, rather coldly. "And I don't feel it would be fair for (child's name) to get baptized since we won't be going to church," said the other.

What the parents were actually revealing is the extent of their own spiritual apathy – and the corrosive effect it was having, not only on their own relationship to Christ, but the effect it was having on their child.

Someone once said, "The first rule of holes is this: when you're in one, stop digging!"

There are many families who have been and are digging deep dark spiritual holes and, unfortunately, their pulling their children down into that dismal place with them.

Listen, God has an Eternal Master Plan! No one and nothing can stop it! But, many will miss is! Don't you miss it! And don't let your children miss it either! Remember, there's a church and a Sunday Morning Bible Study Class near you. Be there Sunday.... with your Bible in one hand and your family in the other.

Hip. Hip. Hallelujah

Saved or Safe
The Death Of Small Children

The Bible states in no uncertain terms that "God is good" (Psalm 25:8) and that everything He does is just and fair" (Psalm 32:4) and it further affirms that He will "judge the world with perfect justice" (Psalms 98:9).

These three statements from Scripture, plus a host of others that could be cited, indicate that we can trust both the character of God and the character of His justice in all matters – especially as it relates to the death of infants and small children who die before they are capable of exercising repentance and faith.

Let's use a simple analogy to consider both the character of God and the character of His justice as they relate to the issue of accountability for infants and small children.

Let's suppose that you are the proud father of a lively, wide-eyed four year old little boy. Let's also suppose that, for the purpose of illustration, you instruct your four year old that every Monday and Thursday it is his responsibility to place the garbage cans by the curb for the garbage men to pick up. Let's also suppose, as logic would demand, that when Monday comes your four year old does not take out the garbage cans. There is a reason why your four year old has not taken the garbage cans to the curb. He is incapable.

Let's also suppose, as ridiculous as it may seem, that when you return home from a hard day's work you become angry about the garbage cans not being taken out. You call in your four year old, express your anger, spank his bottom and put him in a corner.

Question: What kind of a father would you be if you did such a thing? Answer: A pretty poor father? A cruel father? An unjust father? Yes, and you could probably use many additional descriptions to describe how horrible, unfair and unjust such a father would be.

For a father to punish a child when a child fails to do something that the child is incapable of doing is unjust. Such action reveals a defect in the character of the father. In reality, this character defect reveals that the father is not a very good father. It is intolerable and unjust for any father to punish any child or to hold a child accountable in such a situation.

The character of God ("God is good") and the character of His Justice ("everything he does is just and fair), will not allow Him to hold accountable those who have not yet reached the age of accountability.

Therefore, because of the character of God and because of the character of His justice we can rest assured that God has made a provision for infants and small children who die before they can exercise repentance and faith.

These infants and children are not "saved" in the biblical sense of the world; but, they are "safe."

Hip. Hip. Hallelujah

Wounded Women!
Sad Sex

Her name was, well, that really doesn't matter. She could be your wife, your sister, the gal in the next office – she could be you! (And, I might add, this is not a "female only" issue, but for this venue I'll address it as such.)

She was basically a "young" believer, in her late forties and saved for less than two years. She was one of the sweetest, happiest people I'd ever met. She loved God, loved God's church and loved her pastor. She had the ability to wiggle her way into your heart, and she did that often, and with many people, both inside and outside the church! Her joy and happiness were contagious, conspicuous and continuous. Everybody was happy when she was around. She carried sunshine wherever she went, wherever she was.

Then one day…..

Yep! There's always that one day, isn't there?

Then one day….. she came into my office wearing a really "sad sack" kind of face. Nothing fake about what I was seeing either – she was too distant and too distracted and too disturbed mentally and emotionally to fake this dour, sour kind of mood.

"What's up with you," says I. "Nothing." But, we both knew better. "Sit down, take a load off your mind," says I. "I've never seen you this way -- so depressed, so down! So tell me, what's up? Empty your bucket, tell me about it!"

"Well," says she, after a long pause. "I've been reading this book and it says if 'this' happened to you when you were a child, then this is what will be happening to you when you're an adult!"

What followed was the painful story of a wounded woman, a story I've heard often, more often than any could imagine. Sitting in the shadows of our congregations, and, yes, sometimes standing at the forefront, are wounded women who bear a silent secret of the 'this' that happened to them– sexual abuse.

After she talked for awhile I assured her that God's Truth could and would "set her free!" – and it did – three days later!

"So you've been reading this book for four days now," says I, "and you find that what the book is saying is true in your life – you're experiencing these things, negative things, and you're depressed, really depressed about that – down in the dumps!"

"Yes," says she. "Yes, I am really, really very depressed about what I have been reading and about what is now happening with me."

"Were you depressed last week before you read the book?"

"No," says she, but I didn't KNOW about these things before I read the book."

"No," says I, "let's correct that -- you didn't BELIEVE these things until you read the book! There's a difference!"

She tilted her head and raised one brow, not knowing what to say or what to think. "Well," says she as the other brow raised,"what do you mean?"

"I mean that before you read this book you were one of the sweetest, happiest people I'd ever met. You were like that because you were reading and believing what the Word of God says about you. God said, 'You were a new creation; old things had passed away and all things – everything about you – was new and fresh!' -- and that made you happy and joyful."

She tilted her head and raised one brow a second time.

"God said that you were 'born again' and you were and you experienced a newness of life – and that made you happy and joyful! You believed what you read about yourself in God's Word and that made you happy and joyful –and you actually became a new person altogether."

She tilted her head yet again then inched closer as I continued to speak.

"Now, you're reading and believing this other book, a book that describes your old life and the end product of that old life, negative things, and you're depressed, really depressed about that. What that book is talking about is real. These things do bind many, many women to a painful past. God's Book talks about something that is real too, something very real – but it shows how you can be set free from that painful past."

The corners of both eyes began to moisten. She reached into her pocket, retrieved a tissue, then wiped the tears away.

"Choose now, but choose carefully, and

choose wisely. Which book do you believe, I mean, really believe? Who do you believe-- God or the person who wrote this book? What do you believe, what do you really believe about yourself? God says you've been severed from the power of the past and the power of that old life, and a new power, the very power of God has been unleashed and now flows within you and through you. You've been set free!"

Her prescription, with respect to her past and her past experience: "Go home and give yourself a pity party from three days. On the third day, the day of resurrection, believe, know and trust "the power of His resurrection" and thank Him for that power. You have been – not will be – but have already been set free!"

Final note: God seldom removes painful memories, but He can and does heal them as we bring them to Him!

Know this, God can and does heal!

"Turn your wounds into wisdom," said an anonymous poet!

"Most things break, including hearts," added another.

In "Harry Potter and the Order of the Phoenix" J. K Rowling writes – "Some wounds run too deep for the healing." On the opposite end of the spectrum is the old adage "Time heals all wounds!"

You see, just about everyone has an opinion, a thought, an idea – about woundedness, brokenness – and healing. And therein lies the fly in the ointment! Some falsely believe that "some wounds run too deep" – and cannot be healed! While others mistakenly put faith in the passage of time to heal!

Know this! Time heals nothing! Only Christ, only Christ, truly heals! Know this! There is no wound so deep, so hidden, that Christ cannot reach it – and heal it!

Here's another incident filled with sadness and sorrow. Her eyes! Her eyes revealed an anguish, an inner anguish that she could not hide. Though it beat in her chest, her heart was a dead heart! Yes, her heart was dead -- Dead to life. Dead to love. Dead to God. Tortured by her past! Tortured by her secrets! Tortured! Tortured! Tortured! Her wounds, her scar tissue – was real, terribly real – and she desperately needed healing! And, she got it.

No matter who you are. No matter where you are. There is help -- and hope -- for you! Know this – God loves you and has a wonderful plan for your life. He can and He will heal your wounds. Know this –there is a part that is God's that you cannot do. (He will do His part, count on it). And, there is a part that is yours that God will not do.

Listen carefully – not too, too far from where you are God has strategically placed a church, a warm, loving, nurturing, deeply spiritual church family, who will love you and surround you with God's love. And, there, leading that church, is a wise pastor that God has placed there – just for you! Draw on his wisdom, his strength and his awareness of God's healing – that pastor is there – he's God's man -- waiting just for you!

Hip. Hip. Hallelujah

Paint By Number
They Lived Happily-Unhappily Ever After

She was a graduate of Mississippi College, speaking in Chapel, testifying and telling her Life Story. She likened her Life Story to a Portrait on a Canvas. With a flare for words she weaved a story that portrayed each of us as being given a Life Canvas, a set of brushes and various colored paints.

I thought about her the other day and wondered about her and her Life Story! And I thought about myself and my Life Story.

We LIKE stories that have Happy Endings. Whether the story is in a Book or a Movie or Real Life, We like stories with Happy Endings. Cinderella marries Prince Charming – And They Live Happily Ever After! The Maiden kisses the frog and the frog becomes a Prince – And They Live Happily Ever After! We LIKE stories that have Happy Endings.

We DISLIKE stories with Unhappy Endings. Whether the story is in a Book or a Movie or Real Life, We dislike stories with Sad Endings. We all understand, however, that Life and its Stories don't always have Happy Endings. Years ago, the American public demanded that, I believe it was F. Scott Fitzgerald, the American public demanded that he change the Unhappy Ending of one of his novels. He refused! The public protest eventually abated because Life and its Stories don't always have Happy Endings. That's part of life.

We DISTAIN stories that have Unjust Endings -- Especially if we are the recipient of the injustice. We don't like living in a world filled with injustice; but, we do! And we know that some stories have Unjust Endings.

Because the Human Story is FLAWED and MARRED and filled with Disappointing Stories with Unhappy Endings and Devastating Stories with Unjust Endings, we often DESENSITIZE ourselves to the PAIN that is associated with and accompanies Life in a Fallen Universe. We either See with Dull Eyes, Shut our Eyes temporarily or Walk through Life with Blind Eyes. Jesus pointed out this Human Dilemma on more than one occasion -- Seeing, they do not see; Hearing, they do not hear!

Which brings me back to the young graduate speaking in Chapel, who likened her Life Story to a Portrait on a Canvas. She concluded by saying, "I'm painting a beautiful painting and in the end, it will be a thing of great beauty! And I refuse, I simply refuse, to allow anyone or anything to mess with my painting!"

As my wife and I left Chapel that day I remember saying, "I understand her sentiments! She gave an encouraging testimony; but, she hasn't lived long enough or she just doesn't see the darker side of life that intrudes!"

One Day, The Sad Story will knock at the Door of her Life (your life -- my life), or One Day Injustice will come her way (your way – my way). What happens then?

We stand there…Facing Sorrow FULL FACE! What happens then? WE stand there… Looking Evil straight in the eye! What happens then?

When it becomes obvious and we see that we're not going to Live Happily Ever After – there are some things we should know: (1)

The Story is not over! (2) If you're a believer in Christ, life in this fallen universe is the worse it will ever be! If you're not a believer in Christ, life in this fallen universe is the best it will ever get! (3) No matter what has come or does come into your life or marred your life portrait – Romans 8:28 will win out in the end and – through the power of Christ you will live happily ever after! And, that puts a smile on the face, hope in the heart, and courage in the spirit!

Enough Said!
        Hip! Hip! Hallelujah!

A Brown Paper Bag?
The Touch Of Our Tender God

She was once married to a crazy man. Her marriage, filled with drug and alcohol abuse and chaos, quickly came to an end – but not before the birth of her son. Her ex – the crazy man -- burned his brain out sniffing this, snorting that or shooting up. He lived on the streets, under houses, under bridges – just about anywhere – and she couldn't handle that any longer. She had a baby son who needed her care.

"Life was hard back then," said she to me as she came forward while the church sang "Just As I Am."

She related how she and her baby boy lived in St. Tammany parish in a storage shed behind the Winn Dixie until she could get on her feet. Her cousin was the manager.

"Things were hard back then," said she, "but that was yesterday. Today things are better -- still hard – but better -- I have Jesus." She talked a little longer then she looked intently at me. "I have a prayer request," said she. "That's why I'm coming forward. But I don't want to tell you or anyone else what the prayer request is. If I did you or someone in the church would probably take steps to answer my prayer. I want the answer to this prayer to be specifically and undeniably from God – without outside interference. It's nothing big, but, I want the answer to this prayer to definitely be from God."

Three weeks later at the close of the church service she came forward again, to the front of the church, carrying a brown paper bag. He face was glowing. She wore a smile. She gave testimony of her "secret" prayer request and shared with us how God – and God alone – answered her prayer.

Then, with her now five-year-old son standing next to her she said, "Son, show the people what God gave you!"

And he did! He reached down into the paper bag and out came a baseball glove! He rolled his little fist into a ball and began popping it into the leather glove. I can still see her standing there with one hand raised to heaven – "Thank You, Jesus!"

"Amen! Amen!" shouted some folk! Others wept silently! Still others stood, applauding! And many wondered, "What kind of God is God-- Big Enough to create the Universe yet Close Enough, and Tender Enough, to give….

Complete the above sentence
with your need and
make it your "secret" prayer request!

Hip! Hip! Hallelujah!

Stuck!
When You Can't Go On

"I'm stuck," says she; and stuck she was! Two failed marriages, a string of broken relationships, a stint in a rehab plus a long history of missteps and misdeeds. She was stuck, alright, very much so – stuck in anger, stuck in fear, stuck in despair!

Every time she tried to move forward in life, the long arm of the past held her back. Stuck!

"I can't go on," said she. "I just can't!"

That was a long time ago! Today, everything is different. She's a radically-changed woman. She's moved on in life – moved forward – one step at a time.

How's that?

Her first feeble step was to receive Christ. "Repentance and faith," said I. And, she did just that – she turned from Something (her Sin) and turned to Someone (her Savior) – Christ! She invited and received Christ into her life. She turned her will and her life over to Jesus. Then, she took a second step, then a third, then many additional steps were taken – and she took them, one step at a time.

An ancient Chinese proverb says that "a journey of a thousand miles begins with the first step." She took that first step, that first day, many years ago! With the dawn of each new day she took yet another step forward, then another, each day traveling a little further and a little deeper into the new life given by Christ. Stuck? Not any more!

> Running! Running! Running! Always in a hurry – yet getting nowhere! Nowhere! Nowhere! Nowhere! You're……

S-T-U-C-K! S-T-U-C-K! S-T-U-C-K!

> Ever feel as if you're running as fast as you can –just to stay in place? It's madness! Madness! Madness! It's the old Sisyphean effort! But, if you stop running – more madness! Sheer Madness! You're……

S-T-U-C-K! S-T-U-C-K! S-T-U-C-K!

Being stuck is a position few of us like. We want something new but cannot let go of the old - old ideas, beliefs, habits, even thoughts. We are out of contact with our own genius. Sometimes we know we are stuck; sometimes we don't. In both cases we have to DO something.

Rush Limbaugh

Do something? Here's several keys, several things to DO....

Stop TRYING... Start TRUSTING
Trusting Christ!
Without Jesus you cannot do anything!
Only He can get you un-stuck!

Big Texan
Big Heart. Big God.

"Is this Dr. Jeffries from Chalmette, Louisiana" she asked.

"Yes, but I'm living in Livingston. Louisiana, at the moment -- displaced by the storm, you know," says I. She was a church secretary from a Baptist church I'd never heard of in Beaumont, Texas.

"Is that close to Baton Rouge or Port Sulfur?"

"Pretty much, somewhat," says I. She went on to explain that her pastor, whom I did not know, wanted to meet and treat me to breakfast the next morning.

So, there I was at the Waffle House in Port Sulfur, Louisiana, early the next morning when he walked in, a giant of a man. I mean, he was the biggest pastor I think I've ever seen. The man must have been at least six foot eight, perhaps even taller. He was a Big Preacher, a Big Texan with a Big Heart serving a Big God!

"Read an article about you and the pastor's in St. Bernard parish meeting, praying and struggling after the hurricane. Man, the Holy Spirit jumped all over me and for some strange reason my heart broke for you, John, my heart broke for you. Tell me your story," says he, "I read that you were still pastoring the church from 85 miles away! Tell me your story."

We talked, ate breakfast, drank coffee and made connections. Along the way we discovered and discussed many things, things about God, things about our churches, things about ourselves and things about relationships. His dad, it seems, unbeknownst to either of us, was one of my long-ago seminary professors.

He put one of his big hands on my shoulder and prayed one of the sweetest, most encouraging prayers – the Holy Spirit jumped all over me.

Just before he drove away he blew the horn and rolled down the window of his car. "This is for your church," says he. "Remember, God will always supply your need." And with that he drove away.

Sometimes, when the going gets rough I think about that unknown Texas pastor and the unknown congregation he represented.

"Remember, God will always supply your need."

And, inside the envelop? Well, later that day I made a deposit into the new building fund -- $25,000.00 from a pastor I didn't know from a church I'd never heard of…

"Remember, God will always supply your need."

> "To be smart, spend carefully.
> To be wise, save regularly.
> To be generous, give extravagantly."
> -- Author Unknown

Hip. Hip.
Hallelujah!

Winning! Sort of
Squealing Like A Pig

A greased pig, with his mouth tightly tied closed, can make some pretty terrible sounds. And, so too do little boys – who get too, to close to the greased pig! Take it from someone who knows. I've been there and done that.

I was a little boy (maybe ten, maybe eleven) and the greased pig with his mouth tied closed was running straight toward me – making a terrible racket – some of the most scary noises I'd ever heard.

The place? Clay Square in New Orleans. The event? The annual New Orleans Recreation Department playground fair. Plenty of candy. Plenty of games. Hot dogs. Hamburgers. Even a beauty pageant. My dad was usually the master of ceremonies for the beauty pageant.

The big attraction, at least for the boys and girls my age – was the greased pig contest! It was like the country had come to the big city – sort of!

One thing about our greased pig was different, though – the large number of boys and girls (nearly a thousand, if seems) who were down right determined to catch the greased pig – well, they were all determined except for one little fella – me!

I wanted nothing to do with the greased pig. I was there for one reason and one reason only – to protect my reputation. There was no way I could stay home (even thought I didn't want to be there) goodness, a fella could be tarnished for life for doing such a thing as avoiding the greasy pig contest.

The other kids would call you names like "chicken" or "yella belly" or even worse things. Besides, my dad, well, my dad….. So there we were, at least a thousand or so kids in this massive circle of humanity -- inside of Clay Square.

Out of nowhere a man emerges holding a squealing, greased pig. The pig smelled terrible. A gun shot drew immediate silence -- sorta like a sacred hush --then a loud roar of voices, kid voices! The greased pig contest was on!

"Look out," says a voice inside my head. My heart started thumping, and thumping, and thumping. That danged squealing greased pig was coming straight toward me! He was snortin' and a huffin' and a huffin' – his eyes were staring at me! I immediately started running the other way, faster and faster, away, away, – away from the pig, into a massive onrush of boys and girls coming from the other direction.

The rest of this story is hazy. As I ran against the flow of the crowd with the squealing pig and half a thousand kids hot on his tail, somebody's elbow hit me on side of the head. WOW! It hurt. Everything started spinning. I fell to the grown and grabbed a kids leg. I don't know who he was. I just held on for dear life. That kid squealed and squealed, squealed as loud as the greased pig! Wait a minute! The squeal wasn't a kid – it WAS the greased pig! What? I was the hero!

Somehow I had tackled the greased pig! Dad was proud, oh he was so proud. Dad even announced my name during the beauty pageant as the boy who caught the greased pig!

Lesson 1: We live in a world of appearances. Things aren't always as they appear.

Lesson 2: Some, who appear to be heroes, have hearts that "thump" with fear!

Lesson 3: Life has a way of arranging circumstances so as to force us to face our fears.

Lesson 4: (Write the lessons that you see in your Journal)

The Preacher's Game!
The Course Of Your Life/Ministry

The Preacher's Game! Never heard of it? Neither had I! But, for a number of years I played it – and played it well!

Let me explain. College graduation was approaching. A magical time. About to reap the dividends of four years of labor. I had been pastor of a little country church for about four years as graduation approached – when I began to play The Preacher's Game.

Here's how it's played. You're driving along a lonely road, or perhaps sitting quietly on a back yard swing, or, wherever, it doesn't matter – and a holy restlessness stirs your spirit. You begin to think. To wonder About the course of your ministry. About the course of your life. Then you realize that, though you love the people of this country church – you're not going to spend the rest of your life or your ministry with them.

Later, you share the experience with your wife. In the midst of the conversation a question is asked: Where would YOU like to go next? The Preacher's Game!

I remember my answer. "I really would love to pastor a church in the metro-New Orleans area!" And, I remember my wife's answer. "I really would love to have you pastor in north Louisiana – in a place like Shreveport!"

The Preacher's Game!

God allowed us to continue with the good people at New Ireland Baptist Church, in Union, Mississippi, for another two years. From there we moved to Folsom, Louisiana; then, from Folsom to Abita Springs, Louisiana, just outside the New Orleans metro area. At some point, at each church, we played The Preacher's Game!

It was difficult for me to play the game while I was pastor at Abita Springs because I felt that this was the place we would spend our lives and invest the remainder of our ministry. But, then God stirred again in a quiet moment and I knew that this wasn't to be.

The Preacher's Game!

"Shreveport," says she.

"Metro-New Orleans," says I.

Friend, know this, God has a sense of humor! Really. He does.

Through a series of events a few months later the Pastor Search Committee from First Baptist Church, Chalmette (a metro-New Orleans church) came, by appointment, to hear me preach. But, lo and behold, there was another Pastor Searclh Committee there too – unannounced, they came – from Shreveport!

"What to do? What to do? What to do?"

Both churches extended us a call. Both Genny and I applied every principle of Divine guidance that we knew. A decision was made and you know the rest of the story – we're in our 27th year at Chalmette.

But suppose, just suppose that God really intended for Genny and me to go to Shreveport – and we came to Chalmette instead! Would God be angry with us? Would God withdraw His blessing from our ministry?

No! No! No! Triple No!

When we diligently seeks God's guidance – with all our heart – you can be sure He will bless. And, He has! (Read Romans 8:28)

Hip. Hip.
Hallelujah!

Gentle Gloves
A different sort of providence

I was in Walker, Louisiana. Cell phone call. It was Carol, our Administrative Assistant at First Baptist Church, Chalmette. (Have to blame someone! Why not Carol!) Distracted by the phone call as I turned onto Hwy 190 I accidentally cut it a tad too close and hit the curb. Boom! The front tire exploded!

I might add at this point that this was a new car and I had no familiarity with some of the finer features of the vehicle– like, where is the spare tire located? Where is the tire jack? Like the little boy in the children's story I was scrambling on the inside – "What to do? What to do? What to do?"

Now, God, as we all know, provides for all our needs! ALL of 'em! So I said a silent prayer! I mean, get this, before I said

"Amen!" – a State Trooper pulled up! He knew, thank God, where the spare tire and the tire jack were located.

"Policy," says he, "won't allow me to change the tire; but, if you put this end here, and turn this thing there, and be extra, extra careful, that should lift the car."

Well, the jack kind of slipped this way, then it slipped that way. I was working up a sweat. "No," says the state trooper, "put this end here, and turn this thing there, and be extra, extra careful, that should lift the car."

I was like a dazed deer in the headlights. Silently, I said another prayer! You know, this kind of prayer – "Help! Help! Help!"

Now, God provides for all our needs! ALL of 'em! So as I said that silent prayer! I mean, get this, before I said "Amen!" –another man in a pick up truck pulled up! He quickly changed the tire. Shook hands with the trooper then shook my hand and gave me a little business card! "Gentle Gloves Ministry"

"I made a commitment to Christ about a year ago to help at least one person each day! Today, you're that one!" He drove off and I never saw or heard from him again.

Hip. Hip. Hallelujah!

Dashboard Dad
Spiritual Surveillance

1988. Our family was excited! Our son was gearing up for college! We had our short-list, our long-list, our things-to-do-list, our check-list and our lists of lists – do this, do that, don't forget the other! (I'm sure you've been there – done that!)

At some point we purchased a little Volkswagen beetle from my minister of youth for our son to go back and forth to college and to drive around campus.

My wife says I have a strange sense of humor – and sometimes, sometimes she might be "right" . Take this Volkswagen beetle, for instance. Since this would be our son's first venture away from home, on a whim I bolted a framed 5 X 7 black-and-white photograph of me to the dashboard of the vehicle. It was one of those strange, eerie photographs. No matter where you sat in the car, the dull dark eyes of the photograph followed you. We humorously called it the Dashboard Dad!

"Remember, I've got my eye on you, Sean. I've got my eye on you."

"Yeah. Yeah. Yeah," says he, "but it bugs me dad – Dashboard Dad is always watching me! It's like surveillance!"

Oh, one additional thing. I don't know how I did this but once the Dashboard Dad was bolted to the dashboard, well, we never could figure out how to get it off. The car was eventually passed on to our daughter for her college years – with Dashboard Dad's eyes still doing their thing!

"Remember, I've got my eye on you, Sheri. I've got my eye on you."

"Yeah. Yeah. Yeah," says she. "but it bugs me dad – Dashboard Dad is always watching me! It's like surveillance!"

Surveillance? In Psalm 32 God, the Father, says to His children "I've got my eye on you." His eye is not on his children for surveillance but for a higher purpose – "With my eye upon you, I will counsel you" says the heavenly Father, and He adds "and I will instruct you and teach you in the way you should go."

Was my purpose surveillance? No! Hardly! The photo didn't and couldn't provide surveillance. My purpose was simple.

A scene from the movie "It's a Wonderful Life" illustrates it best. A young George Bailey was in a tight situation. He didn't know what to do. Mr. Gower, the pharmacist was drunk, slapping young George around, and unknowingly demanding that George deliver a deadly drug to an unsuspecting client. Young George was in a panic. His head was spinning. He was getting light-headed. As everything around him was spinning, faster and faster, he suddenly saw a sign on the wall of the drug store. It simply said, "Ask Dad! He Knows!" Implication: Sure, I was having fun with the kids – but I really had something else in mind – "If you get in a tight – call me!"

An old hymn says it well, "His (the heavenly Father's) eye is on the sparrow, And I know He cares for me; His eye is on the sparrow, And I know He watches me"- The Father says to His children "I've got my eye on you." Surveillance? Naw! When you in a tight – "Ask Dad! He Knows!"

Hip. Hip. Hallelujah!

Destined For Greatness –
But He Didn't Make It!

Throughout history there have been those who have been destined for greatness – but didn't make it! A friend, Sam was one of those gifted guys who didn't make it. Sam was definitely chosen and called by God – a genuinely gifted leader – a man destined for greatness! Everybody knew that! Everybody was sure about that! Yes, sir, Sam was a man destined for greatness – but he didn't make it!

One thing stood in Sam's way – Dee! Yes, sir, her name was Dee. Sam was enamored with Dee, smitten, head over heels in love with Dee, or so he thought! Dee, however, was a dangerous woman – and Sam knew it – but he was willing to risk everything for Dee

– even his call by God to greatness!

You see, Dee was a devilish women, a dangerous kind of woman, a conniver who had attempted, several times, to trick Sam out of money -- and more. She kept trying, too, over and over again. And, Sam? He just kept coming back for more and more! Eventually, Dee turned Sam against his family, his church family and, in a more than sinister way she tricked and turned him away from God!

Even though Sam hated what was happening he refused to end the relationship. I wish I could share that Sam's story had a good ending, but, instead of ending the wicked relationship Sam allowed himself to be enticed further and further away from his family and God! He fell deeper and deeper under her spell and deeper and deeper into sin!

It wasn't until he was put into prison that he saw the severity of his mistakes and the error of his ways. In that dark, dank prison Sam, like the prodigal son, finally "came to himself." He realized that he had by his own choice "seared his conscience" and that he had by his own choice become numb to what Dee was actually doing to him. He was bewitched, enticed, in bondage – and under her spell!

Even though Sam was destined for greatness, he learned the hard way that his powers, his abilities and his strength were gifts from God – gifts that WERE NOT unconditional! When we're in bondage we excel at minimizing our enslavement. We think just a little longer, just one more time and then I'll quit, then I'll stop, then I'll turn away– then everything will be all "right" . But, that's a lie perpetrated in the pit of hell. What is true is that as we move deeper and deeper into bondage the "one more time" becomes a life-dominating sin!

Ask my friend Sam (Samson) about that. (His story is told in Judges 16) Through his unsavory involvement with Dee (Delilah) he learned the hard way that even though a man is destined for greatness, well, Sam(son) Didn't Make It!

Hip. Hip. Hallelujah!

Sometimes I Sit Here
Daydream and Tell Myself Stories!

The old wooden house, surrounded by large southern Maple trees, was set back off of the dusty road. The place had that undeniable feel of history. Like an old relic from the past the house created that certain sense of nostalgic awe and wonder – awe and wonder about its better days and the people who once lived there. And now, well, the people who once lived there were gone. They had all died, one by one, except for one old man – a 79 yr. old bachelor -- Mr. Anthony.

An amazing wood burning, black pot-belly-stove sat between two huge windows, one on either side of a boarded up fireplace in the front room. Across the way, in the same room, was a bed, a single solitary quilt covered bed where Mr. Anthony slept. And, next to the bed sat Mr. Anthony, in an old rocking chair, rocking and creaking back and forth across a wooden floor. He wore an old, faded tee shirt under a pair of dusty overalls.

Mr. Hezzie Lloyd, my one deacon, introduced me to Mr. Anthony. I was the new pastor, just starting my ministry at my second church in the Village of Folsom, Louisiana. Mr. Anthony, Mr. Hezzie and I talked about many things that day.

"Sometimes I sit here and daydream about Ma-Ma and De-De," said Mr. Anthony, who had proudly finished the fourth grade at the now closed one room school house down the road. "When I was a boy all the old men sat around this here stove telling stories. And, now, well, I'm the old man but there ain't nobody for me to tell my stories to..... Yes, sir, sometimes I sit here and daydream and I tell myself stories."

"Would you like to receive Jesus, Mr. Anthony? Would you like to invite Christ into your heart?"

He stopped rocking, looked intently at me, as one man looking to another man, eye to eye, with a silent stare. "Yes," said Mr. Anthony with a tear in the corners of his eyes. "I would like to do that."

We knelt down, holding hands, forming a circle, Mr. Hezzie, Mr. Anthony and me, as Mr. Anthony invited Christ into his life. Mr. Anthony turned away from Something (his Sin) and turned toward Someone (his Savior). He was saved, born-again, and excited about it too!

"Anthony," asked Mr. Hezzie. "I've been visiting and visiting you for nearly 40 yrs. I've come with preacher after preacher and haven't been able to get you to church – not one time, that I can recall, not one time. Today, I come with this here young preacher boy and bammmm you invite Jesus into your life. I don't understand – what's different this time?"

"Well, those others asked me to go to church. This fella asked me to invite Jesus in my life. I kinda reckon that's what I needed all along – Jesus in my life!"

The following Sunday Mr. Anthony made a public profession of faith and was baptized and, he attended church faithfully, Sunday after Sunday until his untimely death six years later.

"I kinda reckon that's what I needed all along – Jesus in my life!"

Hip. Hip. Hallelujah!

JOHN DEE JEFFRIES

He was blind, legally blind, and couldn't see – other than shadows and dark images. He was deaf, legally deaf, and couldn't hear – other than muffled sounds and unintelligible noises. Nevertheless, he was in church every Sunday morning and every Sunday evening – like clockwork. He would stand when we sang and occasionally shout "Amen!" as the Spirit came upon him.

One day I overheard someone shout a question to him [you had to shout for him to barely hear you]: "Brother Don, if you can't see the pastor behind the pulpit and if you can't hear the sermon when it's preached, why do you even come?"

"Why do I come?" he asked loudly [and indignantly]. "I come so that the Devil will know WHERE I stand and WHO I stand with!" Enough said! Thank you, Don.

Hip. Hip. Hallelujah!

Prologue

I'd like to close this volume as we began it....

Nothing can separate me and nothing can separate you from the love of God! True stories – "truth spoken in love!"

Hip! Hip! Hallelujah!

I do hope God has kissed you through these stories even as He has kissed me! Now, what's that smudge of red on your cheek.

2nd verse, same as the first --
Hip! Hip! Hallelujah!

John Dee Jeffries

Hip Hip Hallelujah - Book 2

JOHN DEE JEFFRIES